I0706399

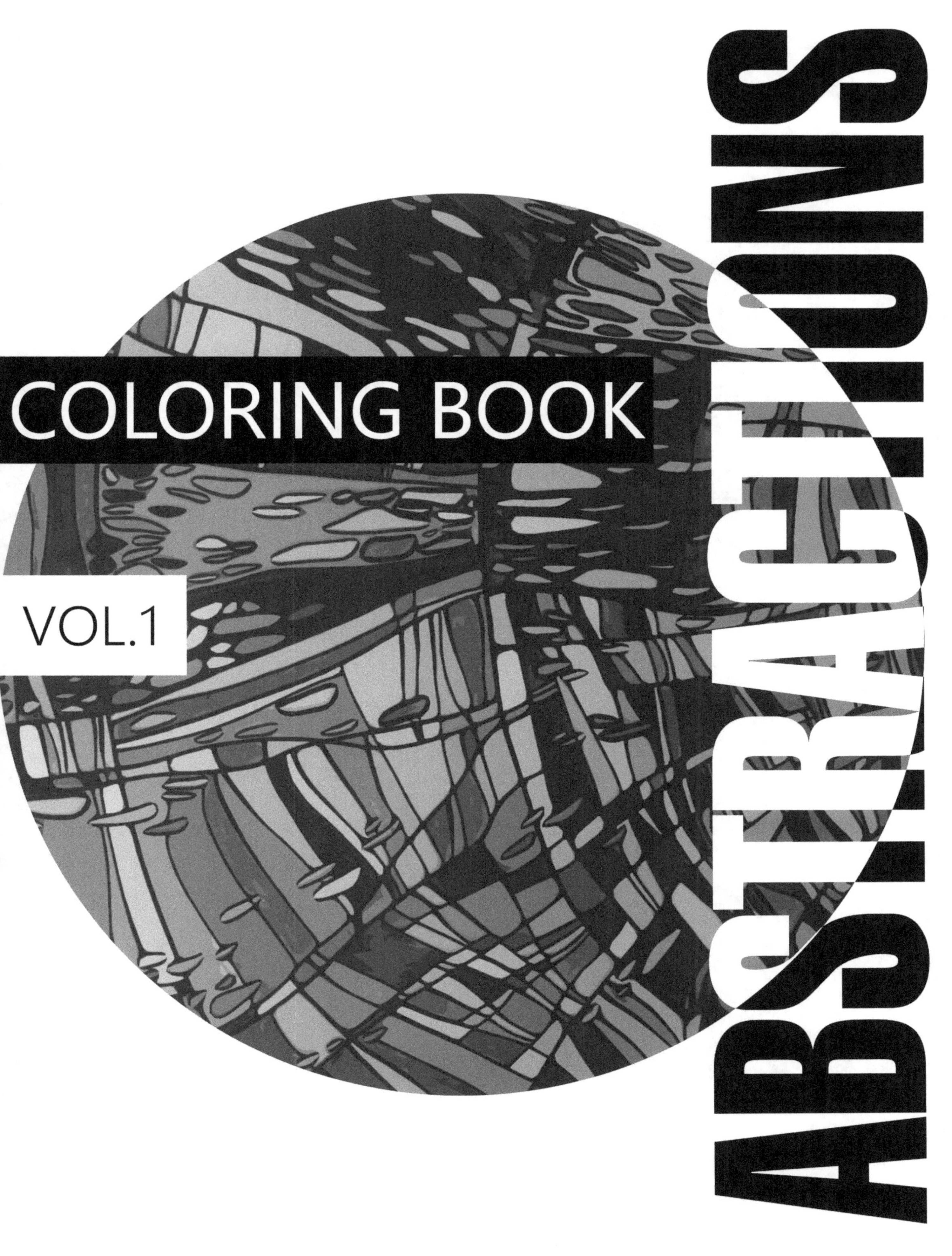

COLORING BOOK
VOL.1
ABSTRACTIONS

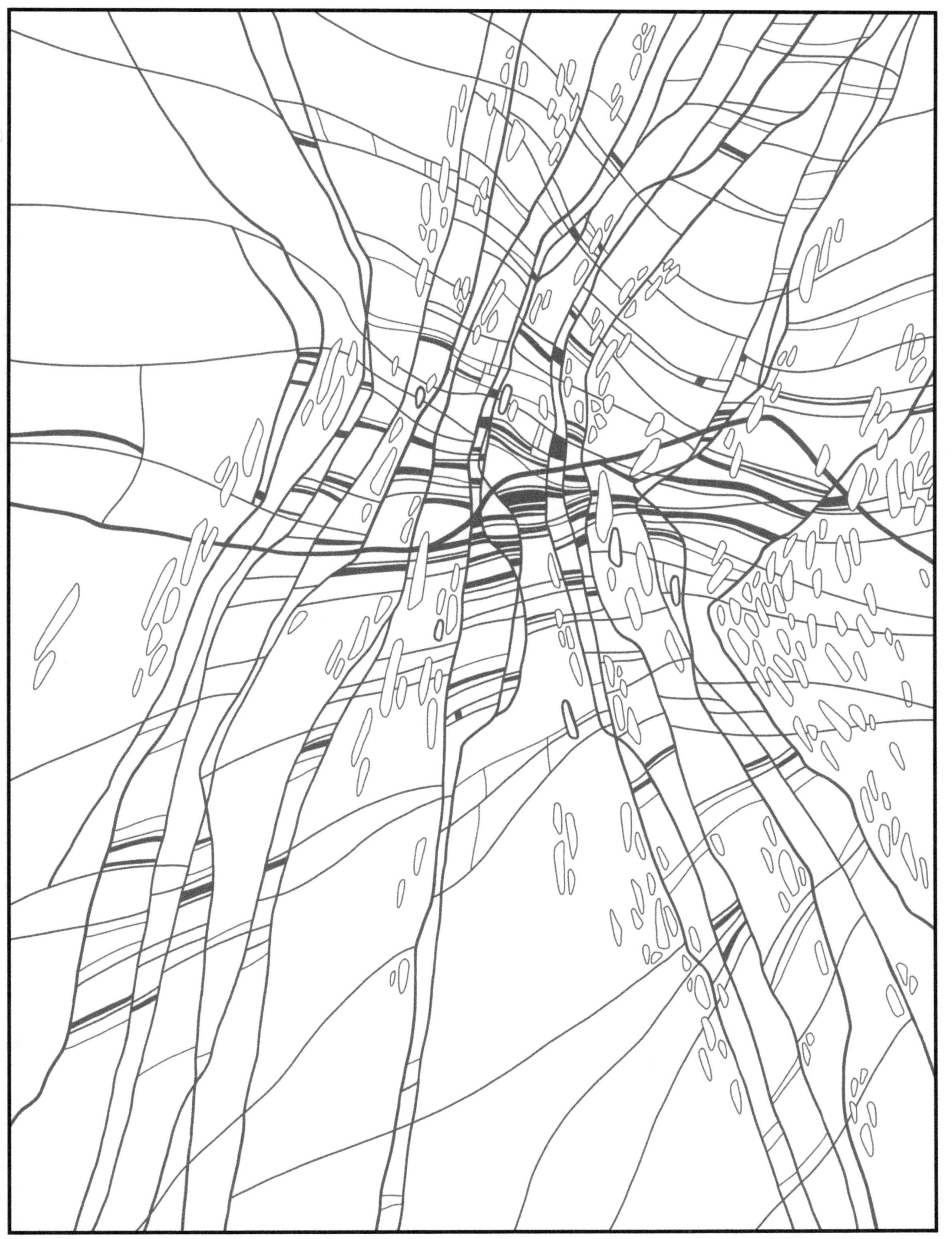

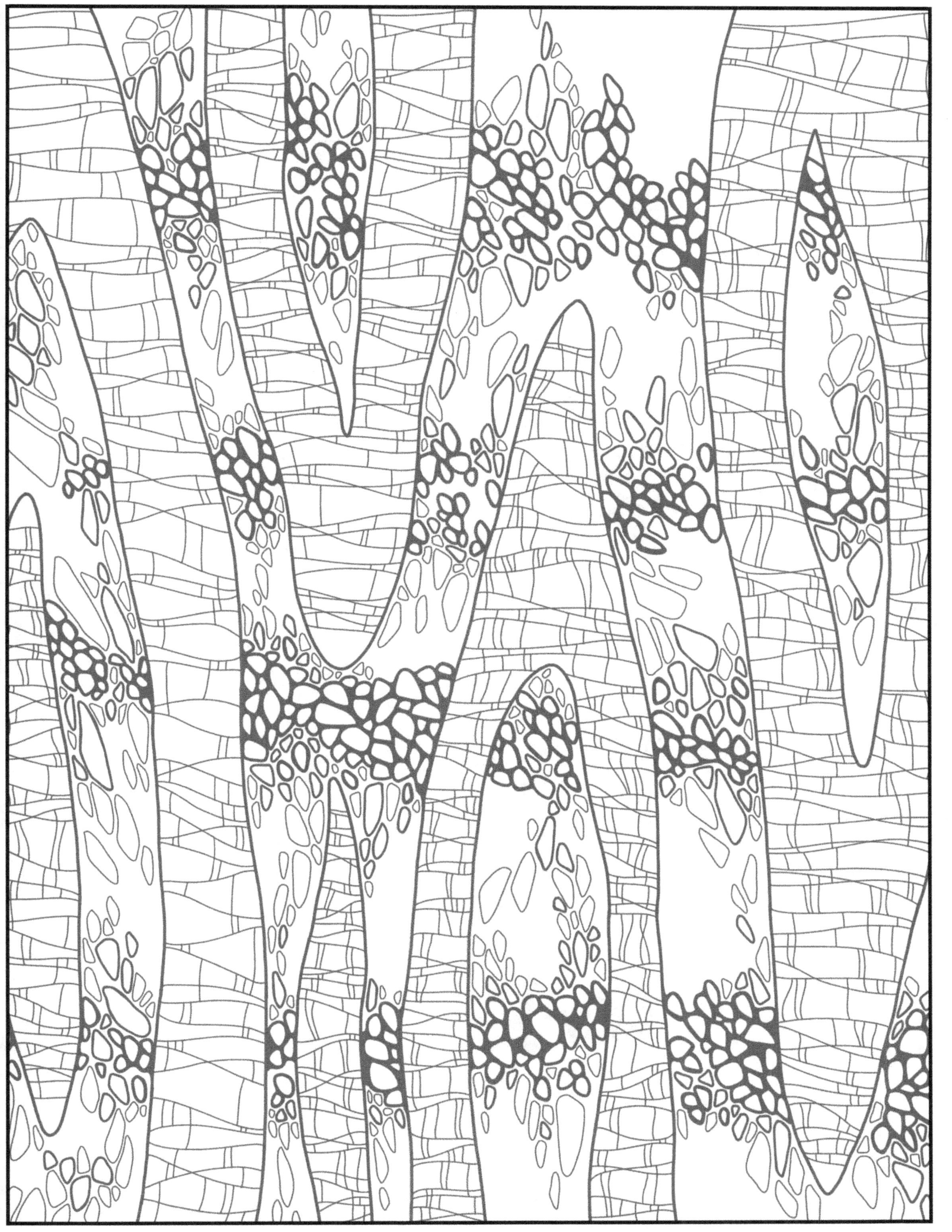

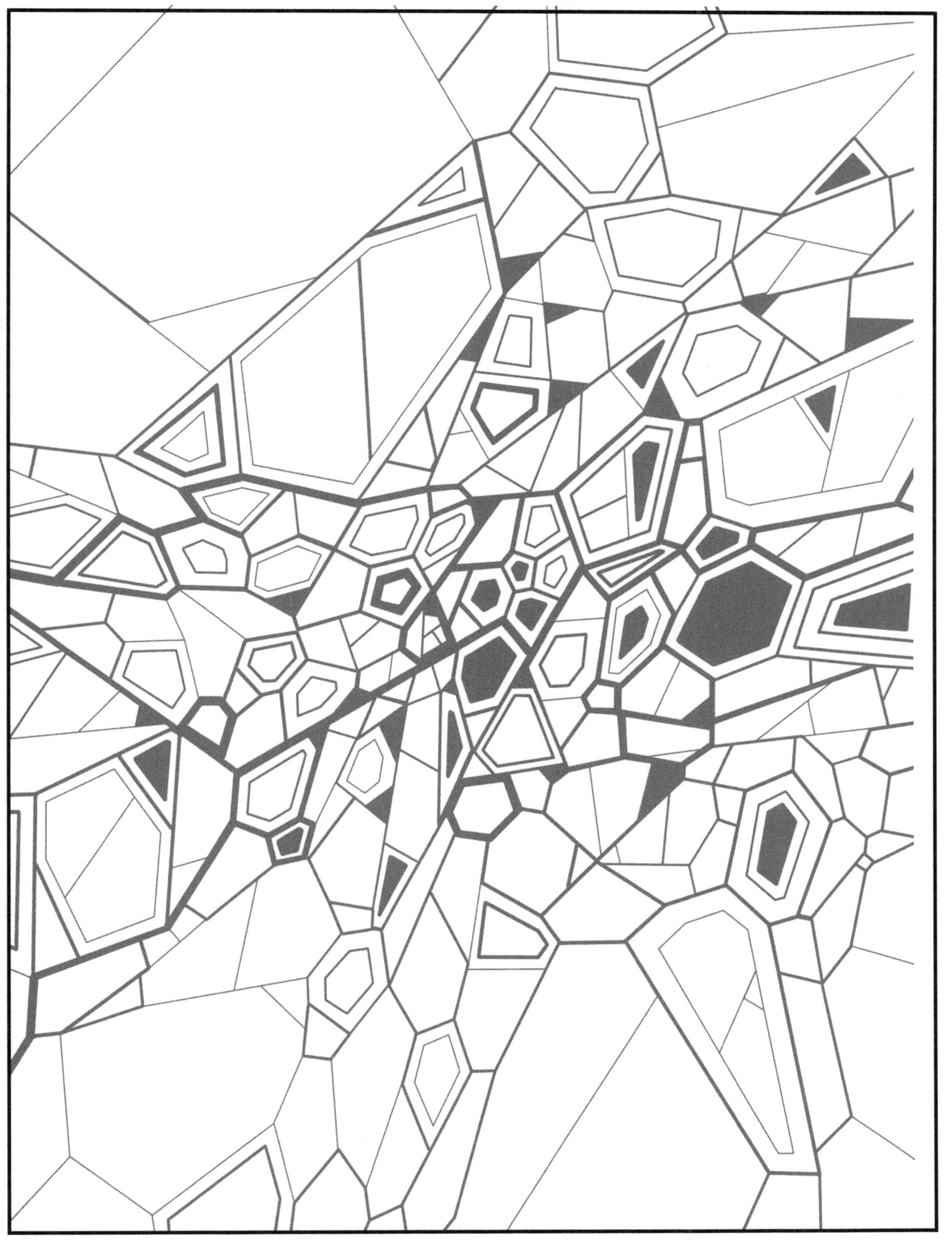

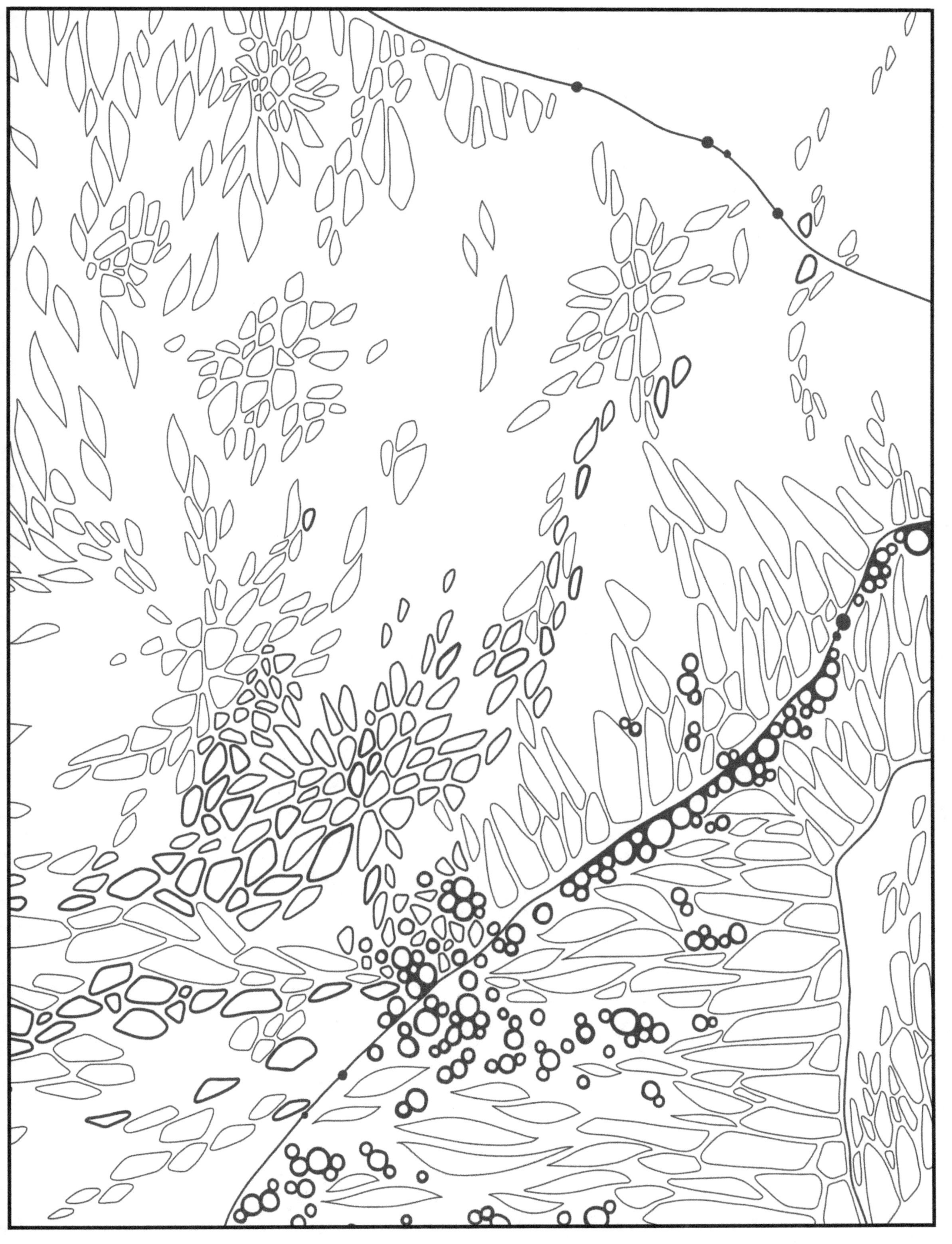

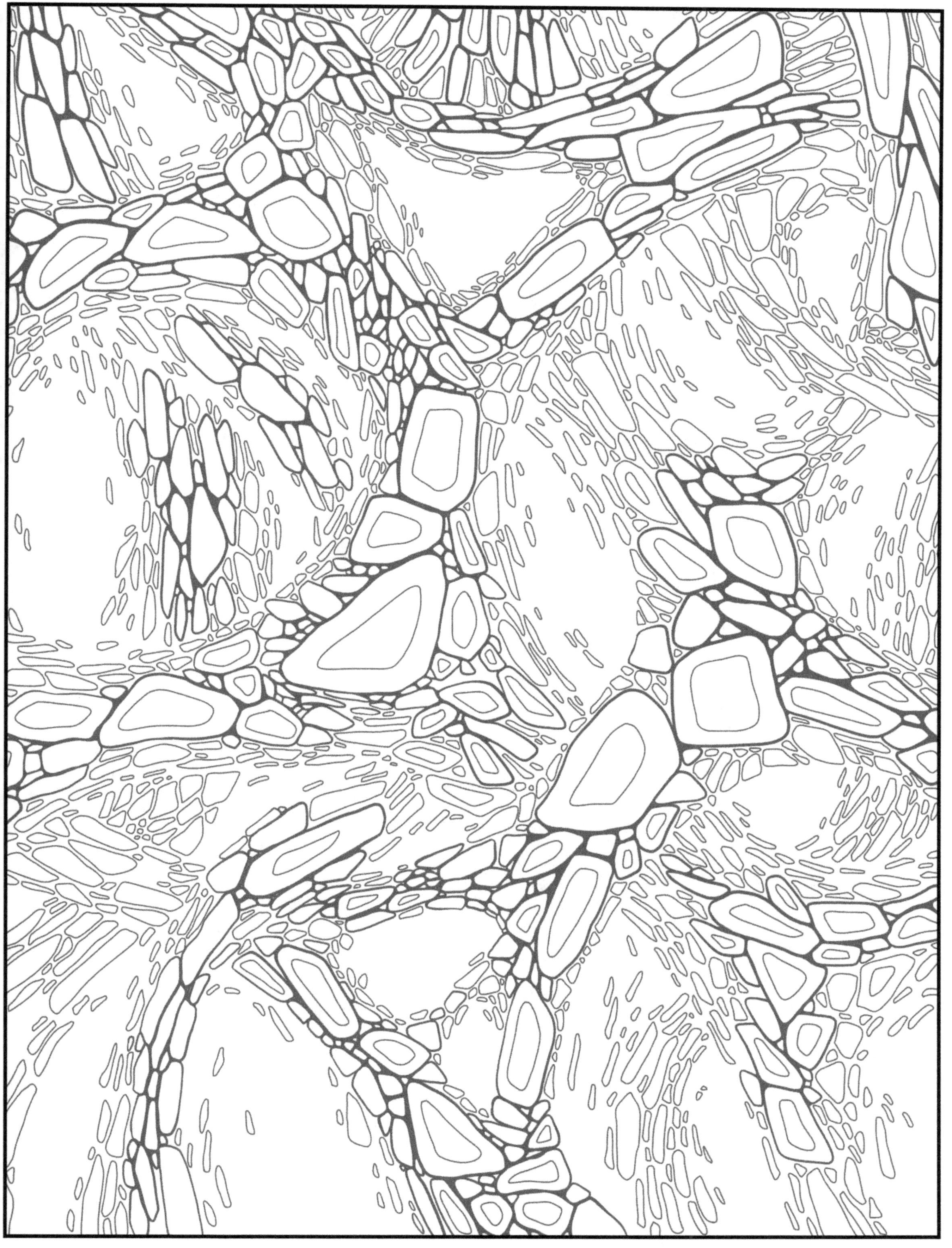

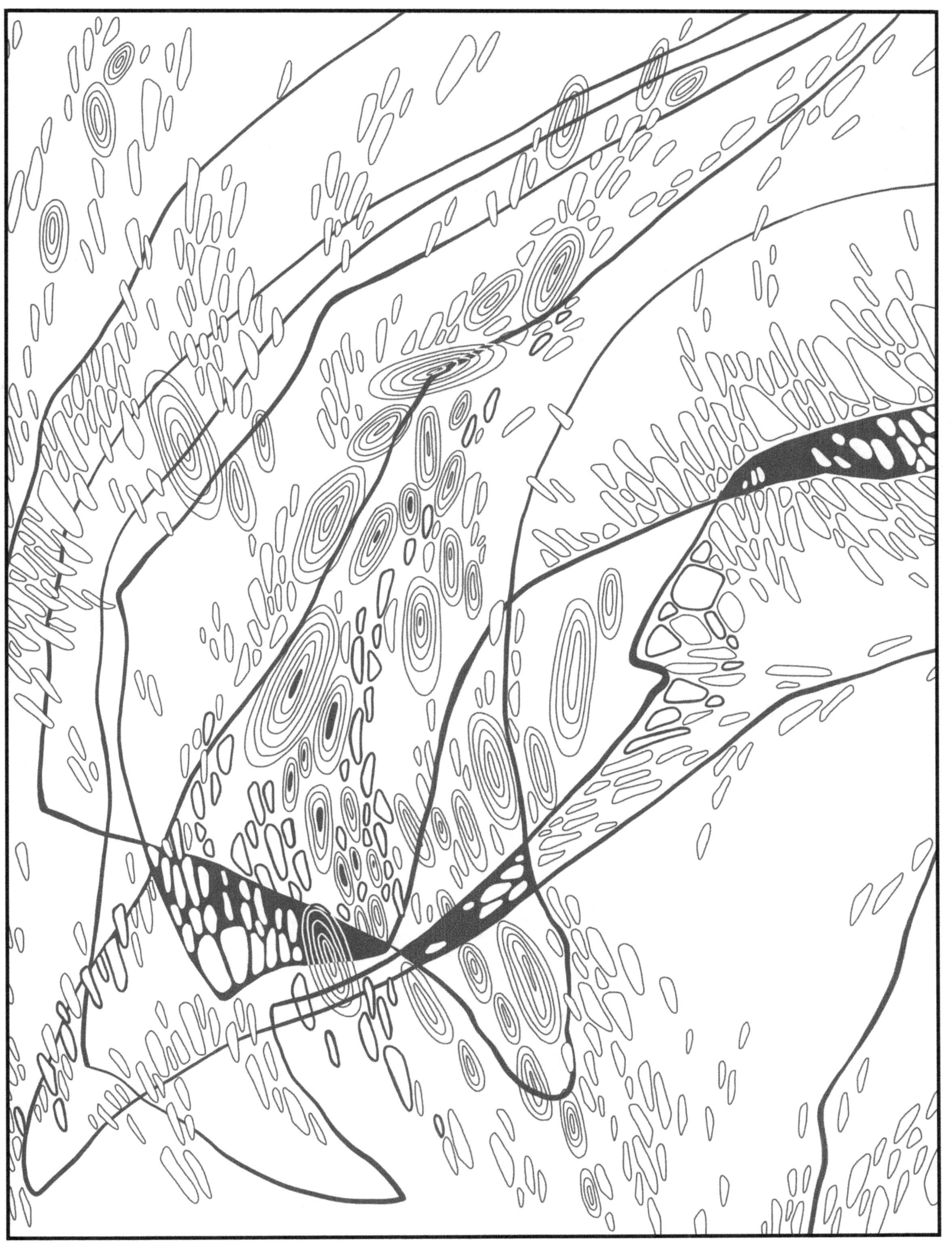

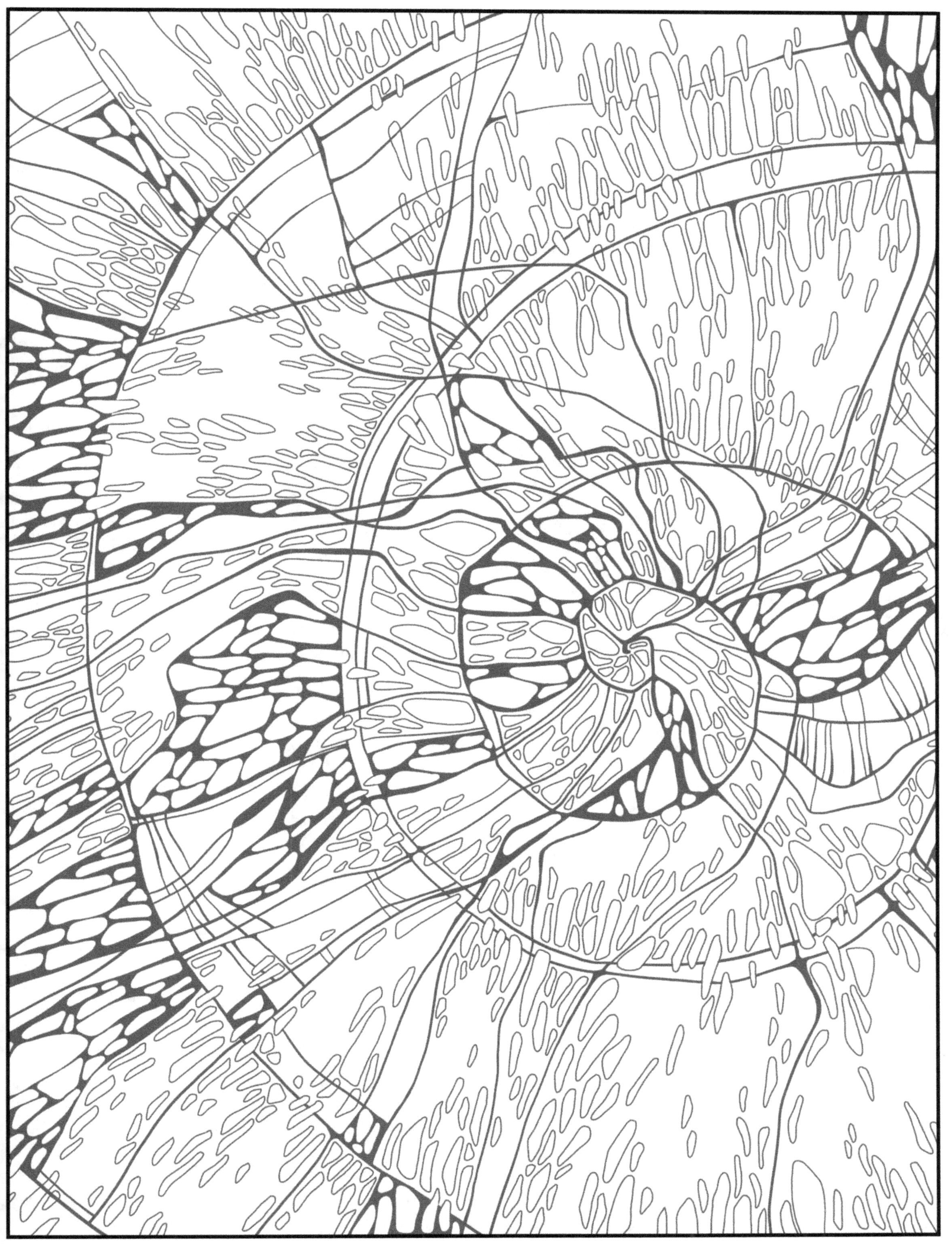

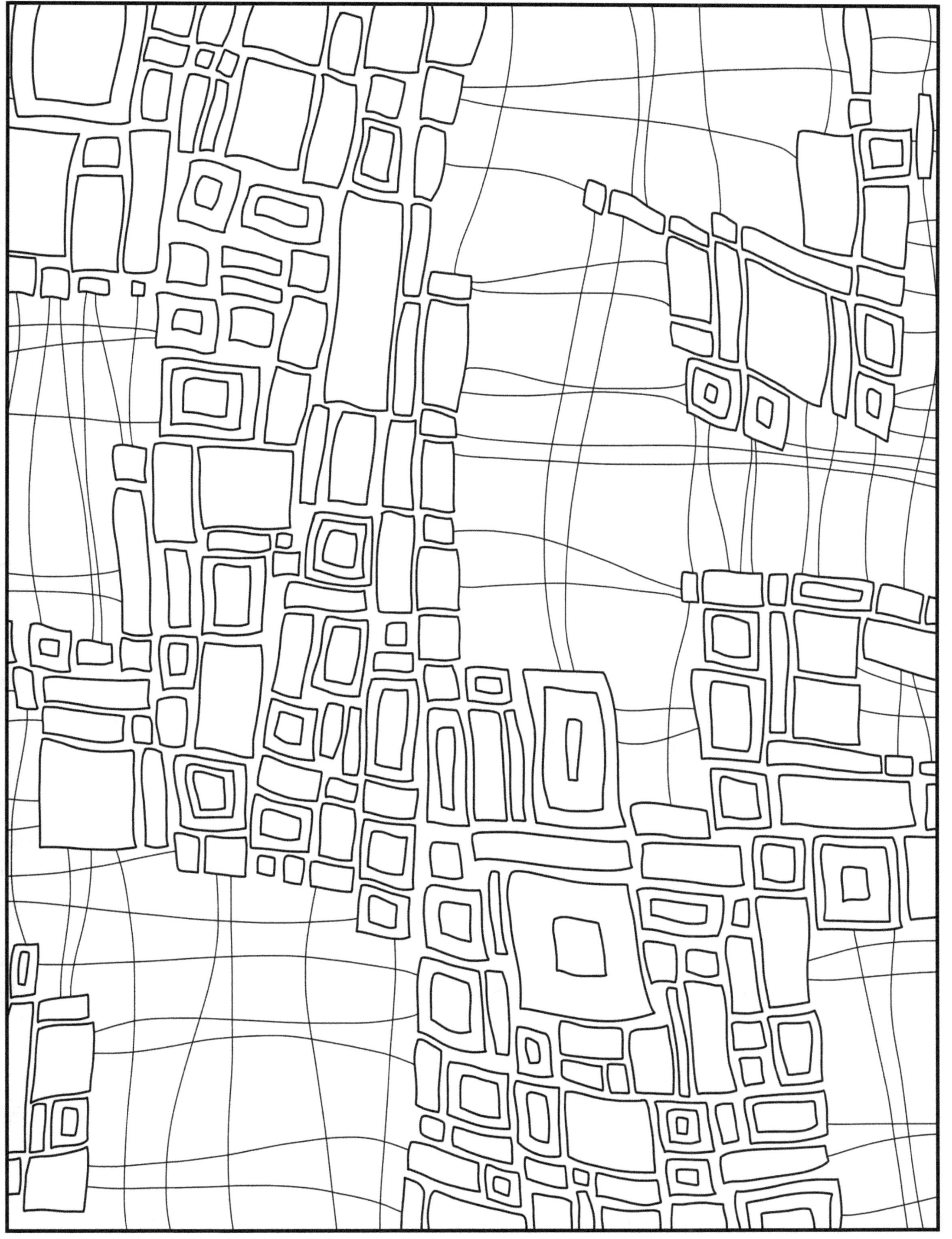

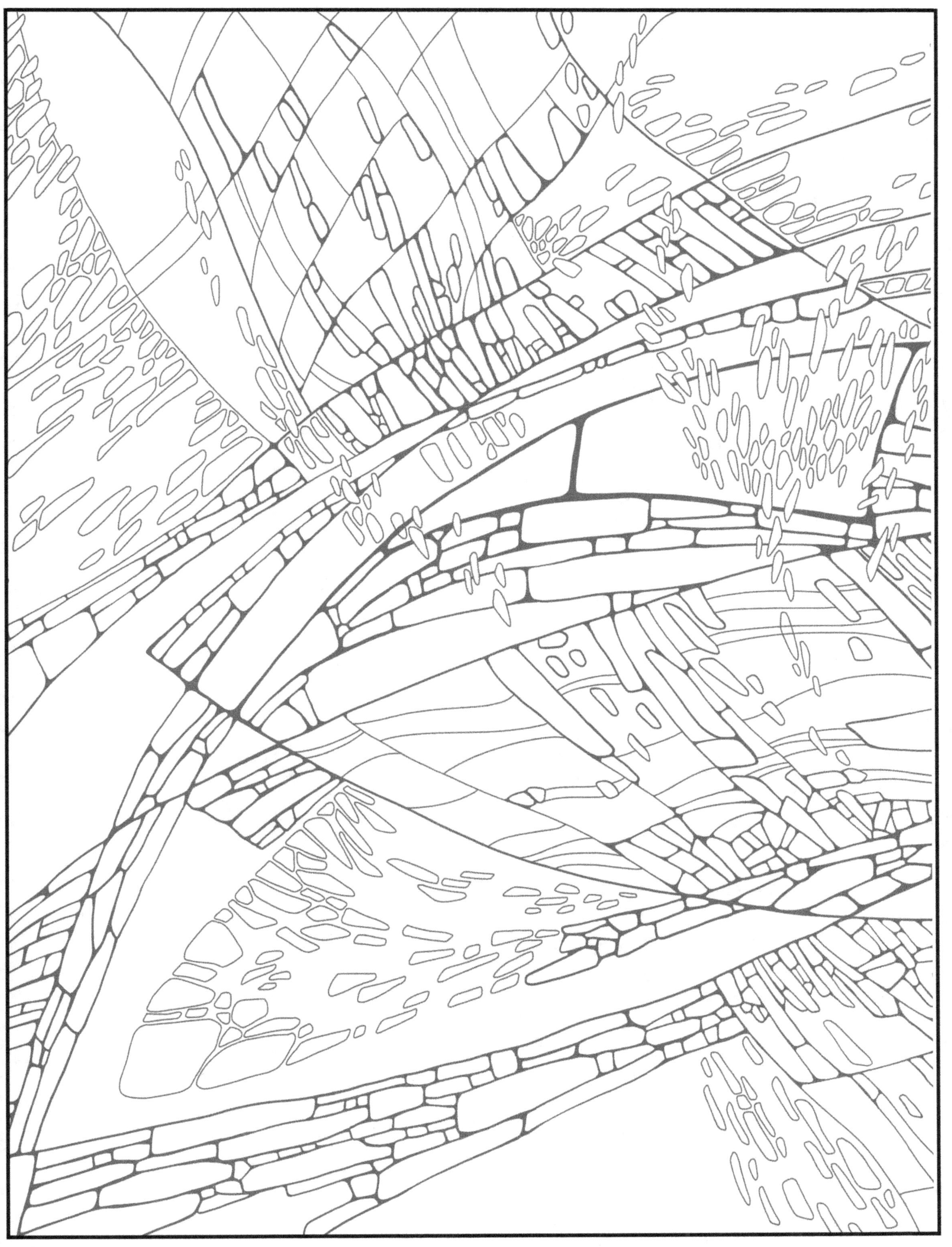

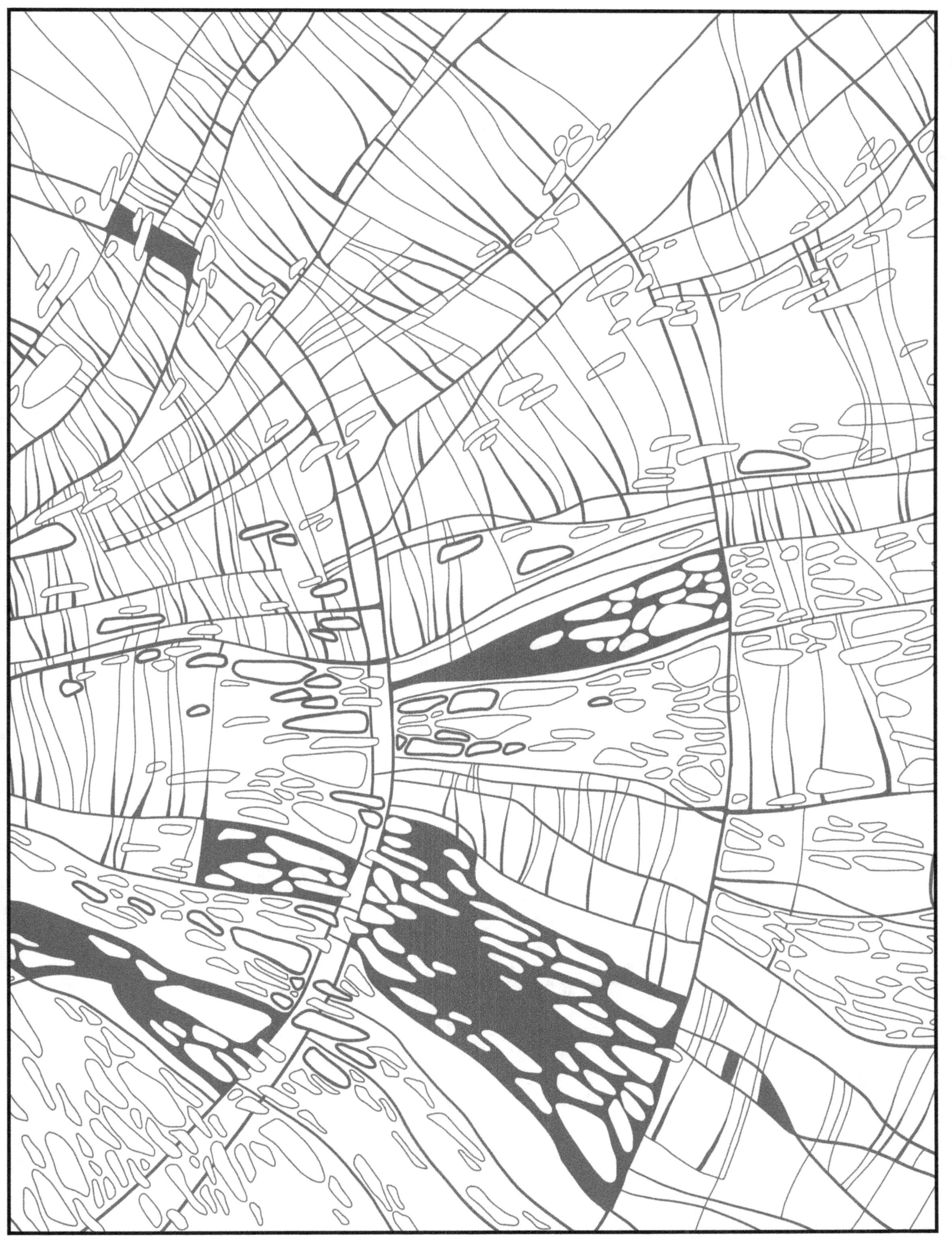

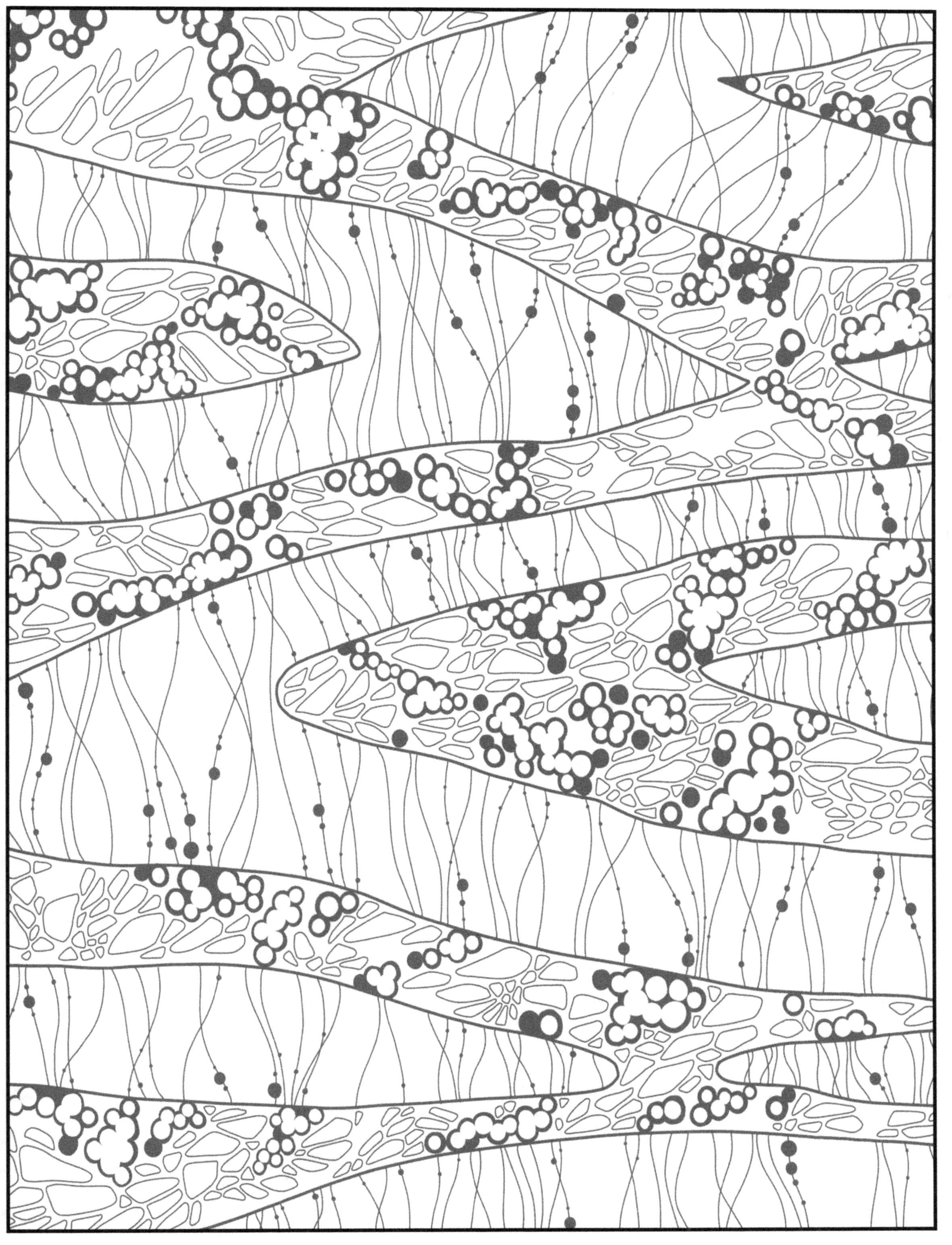

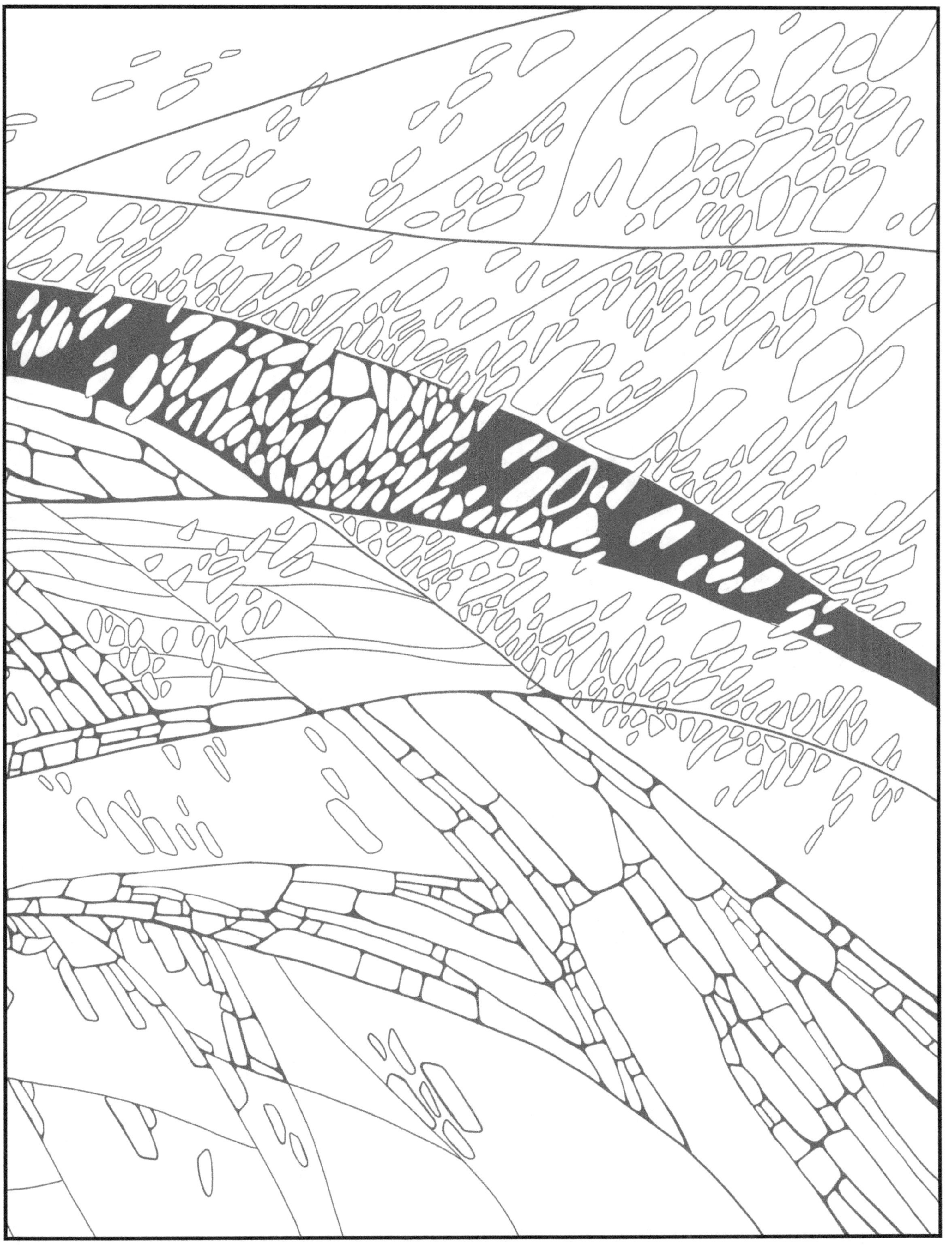

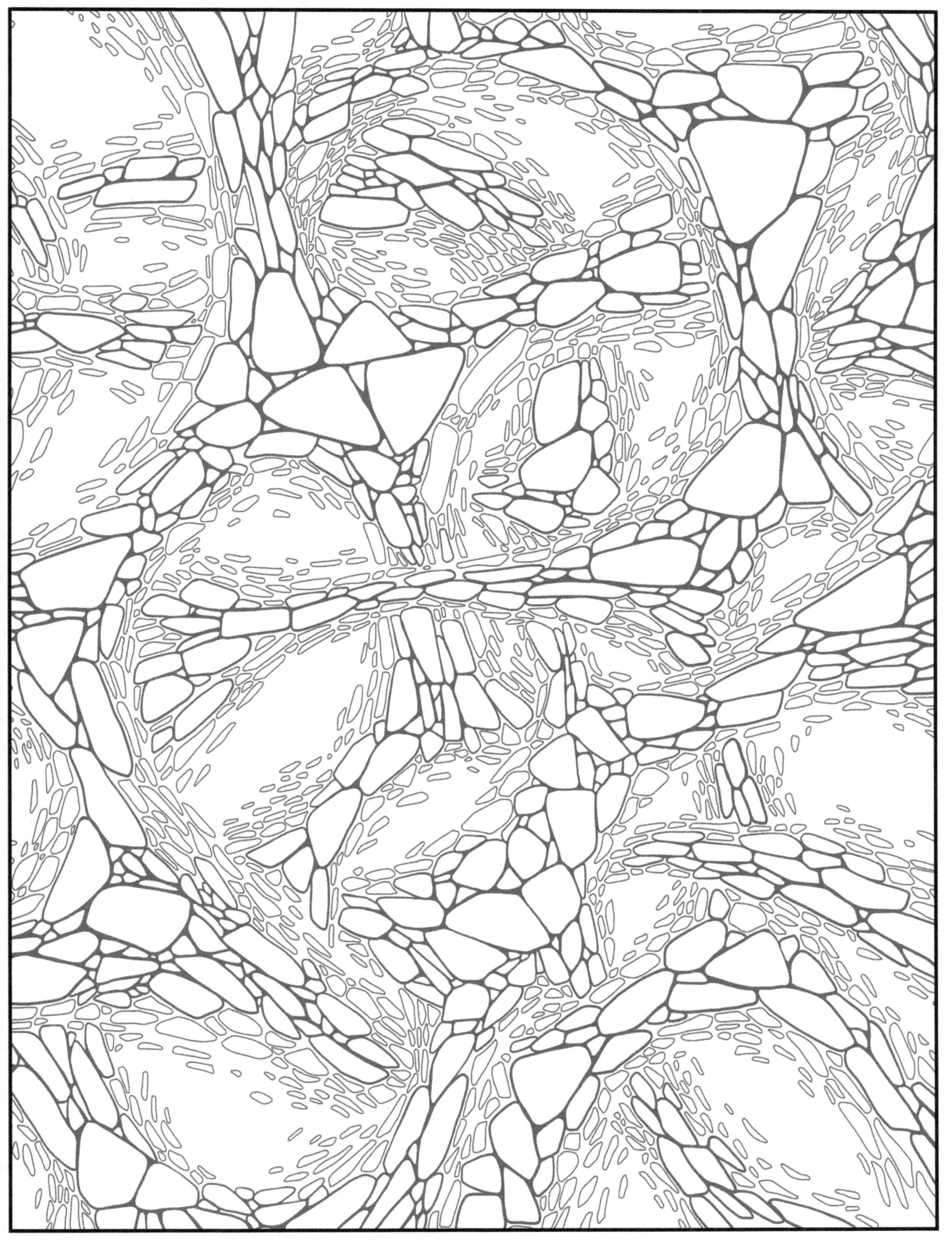

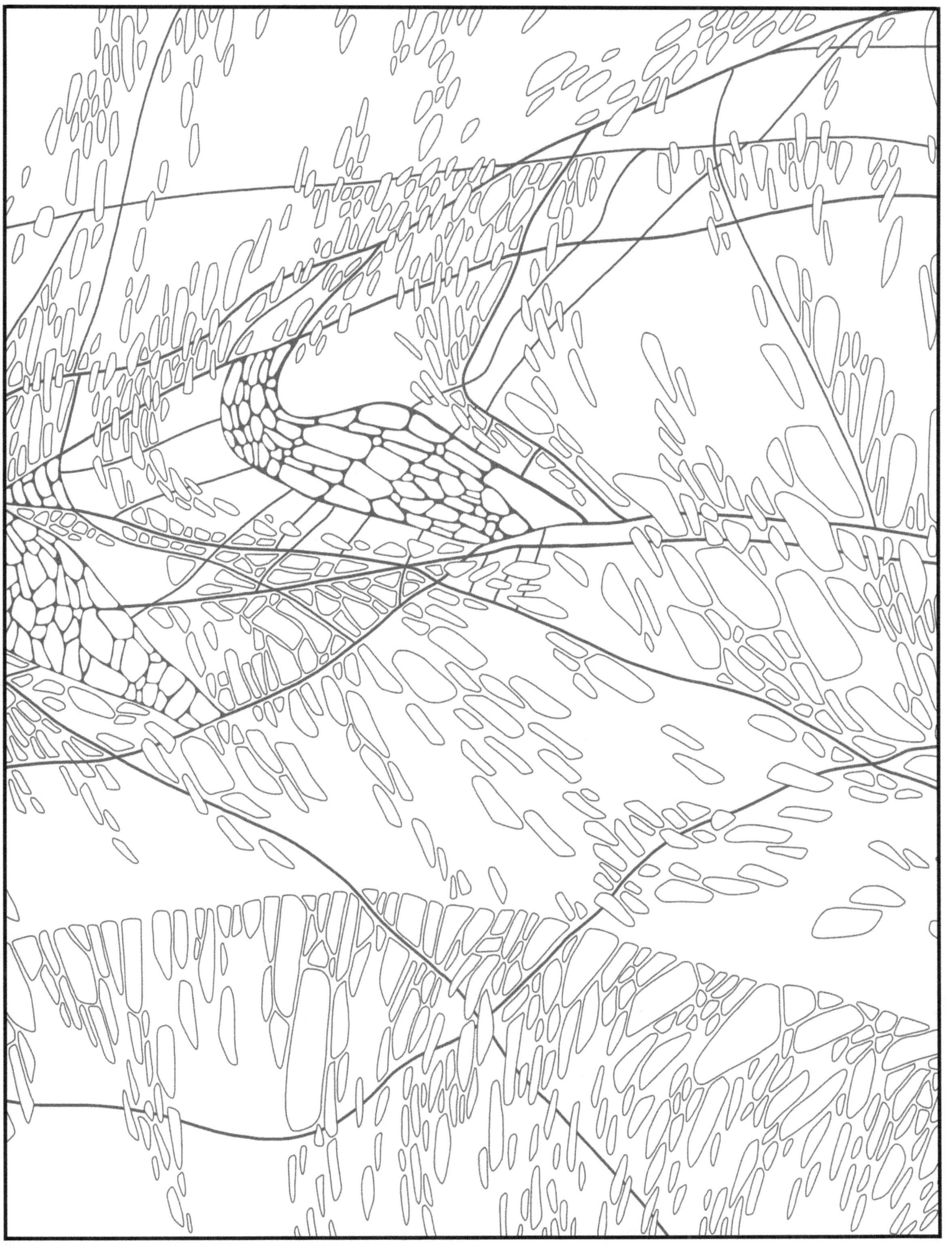

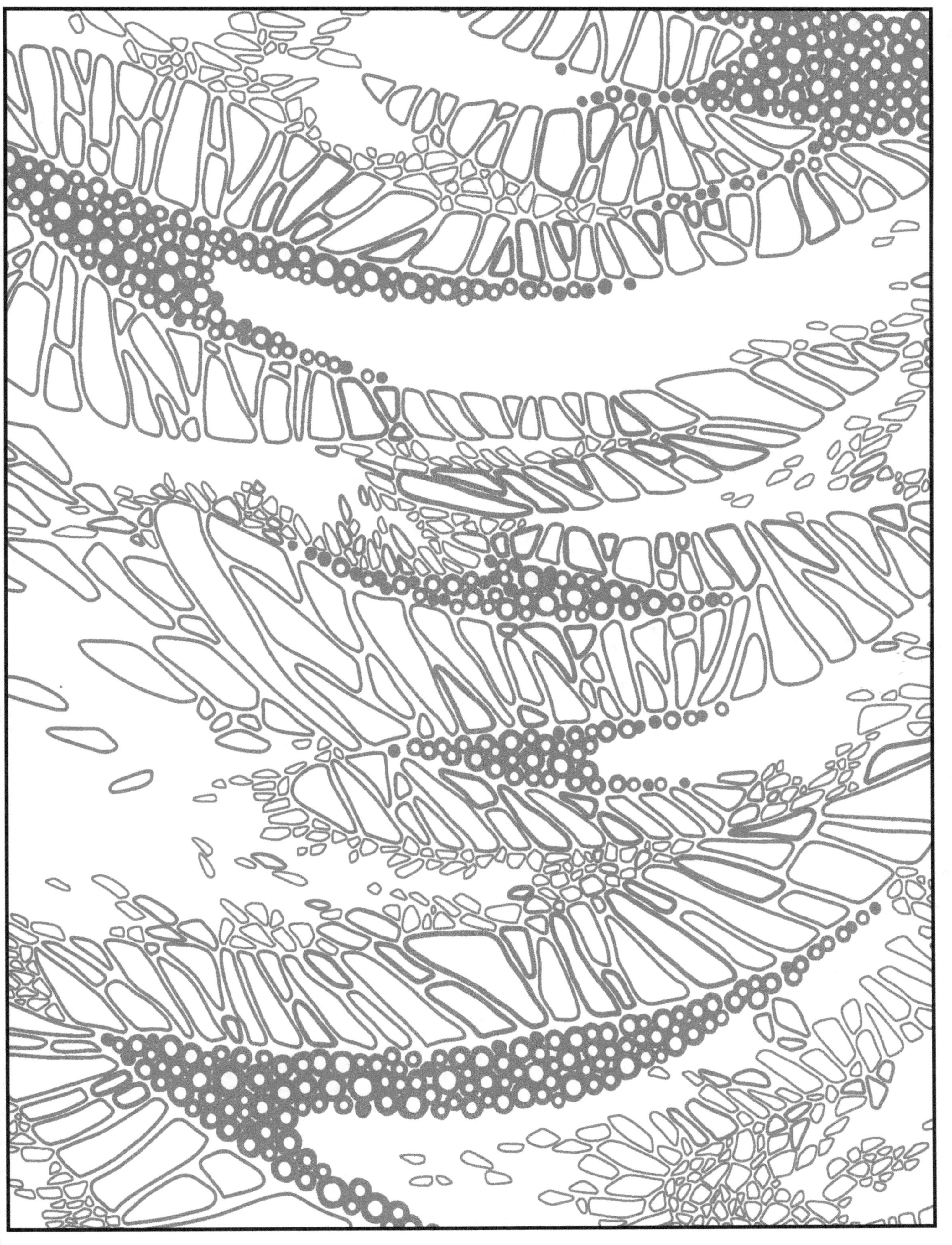

illustrated by
Maria Zapadinska